The Australian Guerrilla:

SHOOT TO KILL

I0022736

Ion Idriess

ETT IMPRINT
Exile Bay

This edition published by ETT Imprint, Exile Bay 2020

Also by Ion Idriess
Sniping
Guerrilla Tactics
Trapping the Jap
Lurking Death
The Scout

The Australian Guerrilla: Shoot to Kill

First published 1942 by Angus & Robertson Reprinted
1942. Facsimile edition 1999 by Idriess Enterprises.

ISBN 978-1-922384-13-3 (paper)
ISBN 978-1-922384-19-5 (ebook)

ETT IMPRINT

PO Box R1906

Royal Exchange NSW 1225

Australia

CONTENTS

CHAPTER I
We Must Fight for Life

IF parachute troops drop on your suburb tonight what can you do? Nothing. The lives of your wife and children and your own life, are worth—nothing.

Should enemy troops land in your paddock you can take to the hills. But your farm will go up in smoke while you and your wife and kids will be hunted like rabbits. For you have nothing to fight with.

If an enemy bayoneted your wife you could neither save nor avenge her. At this moment of writing we are defenceless against this phase of modern "all in" war.

Yet strangely enough, we could be the saviours of our —if only we were organized and armed. Australia is unconquerable provided every man is armed and ready to drop his work tools in sudden emergency to fight and thus take portion of the load off our regular army.

That army may be hard pressed at any time. Should the enemy break through Irregulars must be prepared to fill the gap. Should the enemy still push on, every man in that devastated area will want to down tools and fight. He must—to survive.

I believe the time is fast coming when all will be armed. It should have been done long ago. We will become part of the army, one great army to defend and hold Australia. The V.D.C. will be greatly expanded; mounted guerrillas will be formed throughout the country; dynamite squads throughout every mining district; factory fighters in every factory and in large business and government enterprises. Every suburb, every town and district will have its armed quota.

Hence this little book and the others quickly to follow to teach you the practical use of your weapons in the shortest possible time. And that goes for the regular forces too, for there are many hints in it that they never will find in textbook or on the parade ground.

Australia has been manufacturing rifles and machine guns since the last war. There should be sufficient in the land to arm every man and woman.

The weapons of the civilian fighter are the rifle, the bomb, and the machine gun. In the hands of trained men these simple weapons are still the deadliest in war. We can become trained within a very few weeks. Cut out three-quarters of the drill book routine, and parade ground waste of time. Concentrate on the things that matter, on how to shoot straight, on how to use a machine gun, on how to throw a bomb.

British-Imperial armies in the last and this war have spent months on the drill ground to a few spare half hours on the rifle range. We want none of that; we need our rifles for the most efficient use when the time comes. Six hours of rifle shooting is worth to guerrillas more than six weeks of parade ground soldiering.

With a very few weeks of practice we could handle suitable weapons with deadly effect.

Every male citizen, from the boy of fourteen to the greybeard of ninety, should have his rifle and bandolier constantly beside him. Take it to work in office or factory, out to the paddock or orchard, to the wharves or mine—to wherever he may be. And the wife at home should have a rifle too; she will use it should the time come.

For this is a war where death may threaten on the instant, night or day. It may drop from the peaceful skies, come roaring up the road at sixty miles an hour, come creeping in from a misty sea or dash inland up a river before the dawn.

Regular troops may be distant or stationed in fixed positions, or engaged so heavily fighting for their lives, that they could not help us. In numerous ways in this most unpredictable of wars threatening death may pour in upon us from anywhere at any moment.

If armed, we can instantly give as good as we receive— and better, for we will be fighting on our own ground for our families as well as for our country. If unarmed, we are but lambs for the slaughter and the enemy will pierce in behind our regular troops.

Every man of us will willingly give two hours at least after work each day for training in the handling of the weapon allotted him. And the instructors are already amongst us. Any number of returned men, of old rifle-club men, of experienced sportsmen used to the handling of firearms, of old soldiers who have fought in little-known wars—and, strange though it may seem, civilians who have not fought in any wars, nor been used to the handling of deadly weapons. Large numbers of us in city and town can already more or less handle gun or rifle and very speedily would become efficient shots. There are 50,000 rifle-club members and ex-members in Australia, an army of already experienced shots. Among these men, and among the rest of us, are men fully capable of being instructors to teach the unfortunately large number not used to guns. Doubly quickly these would learn, for we all know how urgent this matter is.

As to the country and bush folk they are already familiar with firearms. The best guerrilla bands in the world would spring up like magic amongst the bushmen.

Give us arms!

We cannot all join the military forces, nor can we all join the V.D.C. But we can form auxiliaries. Form your sections, companies, regiments, from the suburbs, streets, towns, districts in which you live. From the factories, wharves, mines, warehouses, whichever group method is most convenient. The bushmen will form their own squadrons more simply and easily. City men may find Suburban Groups the easier, or companies formed on the block system. If it came to street fighting whole streets would fight. In suburban fighting, whole suburbs would fight more efficiently if in groups or companies who knew one another and their suburbs. Knowledge "of the ground" is a tremendous factor in modern war whether in city or on mountain, in township or open bush, in desert or on winding river. The men who know their city streets and the men who know their country have a very great advantage over the stranger invader.

Form your local battalion into sections, platoons, companies. A section approximately numbers 100 men, under a section leader. A platoon numbers 35, under a lieutenant. A company numbers 200 under a major or captain. Four companies go to a battalion which probably numbers 800 men—or thereabouts.

For convenience and efficiency's sake you may choose that each section of your battalion consists of men living near one another. Thus at a sudden alarm a whole street may turn out and the complete battalion be formed as the men step from their doors. And news, advice, or orders could be passed to the complete battalion without a moment's loss of time.

Make no mistake, an organized people could turn- to almost with the quickness of regular soldiers. And such a support to a hard pressed army would be beyond compute.

If an alarm came during work hours, the case would be different but very similar. Each man would be a fighter even though away from his suburban mates. He would fight in a Factory Battalion, or Wharf Battalion, or Street Battalion, or out in the farmlands or bush squad—just where he happened to be if fighting suddenly broke out around him. If no actual fighting was taking place there, but was threatening his suburb or township, farm or district, he would make all haste back to his Guerrilla Band or Suburban Battalion, as the case might be.

Nothing can be surely foreseen in warfare, particularly in this present warfare. All that we can do is to carry on with our work all over the continent, and be prepared to act and to fight immediately danger threatens.

There is only one proved certainty in this war and that is: given weapons a people can fight and fight exceedingly well. Those weapons will make all the difference in the world to us, our families, and our country.

Elect your own leaders and sub-leaders. It is not necessary that all leaders of a complete battalion should be men with previous war experience. The majority ought to be. The others should be level-headed men who can listen to a proposed line of action, think for and against, then probably suggest an improvement, or a better move still: men who can reason and plan, then act.

Such men in the councils of a battalion could make it very strong. Your battalion may elect a "fire-eater" as colonel, a good soldier who in a short time could train you to put up a jolly good show against a strong enemy. When that enemy came along the fire-eater would be eager to "try you out" which of course would be his job and you'd have to follow him. Well, the job of the "thinkers" among your leaders would be to follow the colonel too, but also to point out to him ways of bettering his plan. The result would be that the battalion would do a better job and suffer fewer casualties.

Remember if war bursts upon your city, your town, your farm, there are going to be casualties. You want as many as possible of them to be on the enemy's side.

I have seen quite a lot of war, practically four years in the front line. And every time it was the level-headed colonel, or the colonel with cool, thoughtful advisers who gave the enemy the hardest knocks while suffering the fewest casualties. So choose your leaders well. We may and will have to fight as scattered individuals, as scattered sections, or platoons, or companies, or battalions, or Guerrilla Bands. Your success and your life depend upon how your leaders have trained you, no matter whether you find yourself fighting alone or with the tiny section, or the entire battalion—perhaps in company with a far flung line of battalions.

Hence, choose your leaders carefully. Avoid the old-time sarg-major stuff, that belongs to the parade ground of old-time soldiering. No matter whether you are one of the Auxiliaries, or a "trammy", or the manager of a great business, you are a worker whose precious spare hours are being given to training to fight for your home and country. And every minute of that precious time must be devoted to the things that really count: to the better handling of a weapon, to the learning of fighting craft that will make you and your section and platoon and company and battalion a better fighting unit in team work.

As you train into a dangerous fighter so your section will grow into a dangerous fighting section. So with the platoons and companies, until your whole battalion becomes a fighting unit to be reckoned with.

If populated Australia becomes thick with such battalions and the bush with mounted regiments then we need not fear. Should the enemy infiltrate, as of course he will, then let him do so if we are not there to stop him—there is plenty of country. But we will infiltrate behind him. Our great continent is so built that two can play at the same game. Should an enemy break through the regular army he would find us everywhere; he could never take us, never beat us.

If the leaders of your battalion are the right men, there should be no waste time. Every moment, step by step, should be devoted to the things that count. During the day the leaders will plan out the programme for the evening, the teaching for every platoon, for every man. It will mean a lot of extra work for those leaders, but then their hearts, like yours, will be in the job.

CHAPTER II
The Rifle

THE rifle is a deadly weapon. In the hands of a marksman it still is one of the deadliest weapons in warfare. It is the easiest to come by, and is a one man weapon. It will be the weapon of large numbers of the Regulars, and of the Auxiliaries.

Learn to shoot straight. That is the one thing that counts. Every man will treasure his rifle, for at any moment it may save his life, a fact that the regular soldier fully realizes. The auxiliary soldier, if his leaders plan their job well, will within a few hours learn the few axiomatic principles of his rifle, and realize the necessity of keeping it clean and ready for instant action. The main thing he must really work for is to learn to shoot straight. As he will be in deadly earnest about this he should master the art quickly indeed.

First, realize the tremendous fighting power of the rifle. By you and your comrades first understanding your weapon you become not only better soldiers but your battalion becomes a fighting power to be reckoned with. You cease to be a loosely strung mob of auxiliary pot-shotters; you develop into a fighting battalion capable of holding up an enemy battalion. But at the same time, by virtue of being guerrilla and understanding guerrilla tactics, you hold the immeasurable advantage of being able to split up into fighting groups, then of coming together again as the action demands. If we thus increase the efficiency of every battalion of the Auxiliary Army then an enemy will soon find he has bitten off more than he can chew.

A poor rifleman would only kill an enemy by luck or accident, even at fairly close range. At 500 yards such a rifleman might fire 1000 shots and not hit his man. And if that man were a slightly better shot, he would kill the poor rifleman.

A battalion of poor rifle shots could be wiped out by fifty trained rifle shots.

Thus, if you get up against a better rifle shot than yourself then out you go—for keeps. If your battalion of 1000 men get up against a few better rifle shots then out the whole battalion goes—for keeps.

Moral. Learn to shoot straight. Then learn to shoot straighter still at varying distances under varying conditions. It will then be you who will live to tell the tale and fight another day. And exactly in proportion as you live and fight so will your families and country be safer, and the enemy's man power dwindle away.

A good rifleman may kill his man first shot, or he may kill him in ten. He and his mates are then safe at least from that man, and he has only used up ten bullets. So that ammunition does not worry him for the present. If he were a poor shot and had lived long enough to use up 1000 rounds, then ammunition would worry him for the enemy may appear all around him and most of his ammunition will have gone.

It is not always possible to hurry ammunition to a regular firing line. Groups or sections or platoons or individuals of an Auxiliary Force may find themselves fighting under conditions where the only ammunition the individual can depend upon is what he carries in his own bandolier.

Hence, a good shot not only saves his life by shooting his enemy quicker, he also saves his life a second and third and fourth and fifth time by still having sufficient ammunition to shoot other enemies as they may appear. Think it out for yourself. There are numerous reasons why you should become a crack shot as quickly as possible.

Imagine your complete battalion in action. They are poor shots, each man uses up one hundred bullets before he kills or cripples a man. Thus the battalion has used up 10,000 bullets to put one hundred of the enemy out of action, By that time the enemy, if better shots, have just about wiped out the battalion—unless it is holding a prepared position where ammunition previously has been stacked.

Actually, if the battalion knocked out a hundred of the enemy for 10,000 bullets it would be fair shooting according to the statement that it takes a ton of lead to kill a man. Which proves what poor shots the armies of the world really are. Hence, if every individual of every battalion of an auxiliary army concentrated on becoming a good rifle shot then battalion for battalion they would actually be superior in fire power to a regular army.

Auxiliary Forces organized and trained only in those few things that matter would become of tremendous value to their country, and to our regular army. The regulars of course would have the artillery and tanks and planes. Working in conjunction with efficient Auxiliaries throughout the continent the country would become impregnable.

I have stated that the battalions in any regular army are, on the average, poor shots. That statement is true because the authorities have always begrudged ammunition for firing practice. Hence the full striking power of the soldier is not developed.

For our Auxiliaries we must insist on abundant ammunition for firing practice. This country has been turning out ammunition for years past; now new factories at vast cost to us are turning out ammunition at high pressure, turning it out in shiploads. Hence we should have abundant ammunition to defend our own homes and country.

Forty thousand Boer farmers held up the might of the British Empire for three hard years simply because they were armed with rifles which they knew how to use. From boyhood each man had had practice by shooting the game which gave him meat.

Any man can learn how to shoot straight. First grasp the reason for a few very simple rules then get into practice straight away.

Any man among us is capable of seeing a man's head resting on the skyline 1000 yards away. So our eyesight is all right, no need to worry about that. The next thing to cultivate is a steady mind which to a great degree masters steady hands and body.

Let me explain a bit what steadiness means. It is that, on the instant of firing, your rifle sights are movelessly in direct line with the target. If it be a man's head then it will be a very small target at 1000 yards. But if the range be correct and the sights be movelessly and perfectly aligned then the bullet will hit its mark.

If not you can fire 1000 shots and never hit the mark.

It is a simple, a perfectly natural result. If you have a sheet of paper then put two dots upon it wide apart. You can connect those two dots by means of a ruler. Align your ruler perfectly and movelessly then draw a perfectly straight line along it. And you have connected dot with dot. But if your hand trembles then the ruler moves just slightly and your line misses the dot.

Well your rifle is the ruler and the invisible line speeds from the rifle muzzle to connect the dotted target. Hence, it is not eyesight alone that makes a crack shot, but steadiness of hand and body as well.

Realize those two simple facts and you are far on your way to becoming a crack shot. Then follow up with a little prac-tice on the range and you find yourself beginning to know your rifle. Soon after that and you will be a crack shot.

A man's rifle is like his dog, his horse. Dogs are dogs, horses are horses, but every animal even of the same breed is very different. So with a rifle. It is the same as any other rifle of the same brand but it is still different, it has its own indiv-idual ways. That is why keen rifle shots love a favourite weapon. They know it, know its ways, know its feel, know its little peculiarities. They will always shoot better with that rifle than with any other weapon.

If your rifle is thoroughly tested for you (which the section leader must insist upon) and proved accurate, then cling to that weapon. Don't change it if you can help it for it will soon become "part of you" and will do good work for you. Every man of the Auxiliary Forces should insist that his rifle is tested for perfect accuracy before it becomes his especial weapon.

Thus, steadiness is of vital importance to a rifle shot, your life will depend again and again upon steadiness under all manner of breath-taking conditions immediately you come into action.

I have said that to cultivate a steady mind practically means that already you are master of a steady body. Let us prove that statement. Under stress of excitement the uncontrolled mind is liable to race, which causes the heart to beat faster, the hands to twitch or tremble, the body muscles to quiver a bit. The nerves do it, the mind warns "danger!" and the nerves react with a consequent excitement and probable unsteadiness of the limbs.

Hence if at a sudden alarm you raced out into the street to find a parachutist just on the point of landing, your first shot would probably miss him. Then you'd fall a victim to his Tommy gun. If an enemy came on you suddenly at night out in the open, you would miss him when you flung your rifle up and pulled the trigger. That is, if you do not possess "steady nerves", which really is mind control.

Hence, in your daily work, in moments of bad temper or excitement, practise mind control. Just remember it often and it will become subconscious. It won't stop you shaking under sudden excitement but a second later it will, if only you've remembered it enough. Your heart may keep on hammering for a while but you'll lift your rifle with a much steadier hand, your breathing almost instantly becomes controlled, you have the power then to take what is called a "cool aim".

And it is the cool aim which hits your enemy before he hits you.

I've seen this mind control (call it what you like) exercised by many a man many a time in the firing line. Just walked along coolly under hot fire (because under the circumstances there was absolutely nothing else to do), just walked quietly along showing no excitement whatever. It has happened to me. And I have been so scared that I've wished the ground would open up and swallow me.

That automatic mind control has saved many and many a man from showing fear when under hot fire. It comes naturally after a time if you come to cultivate it, and this is what makes the deadly shot when under fire. He is thinking only of his target and of hitting it; his mind is concentrated on that one job.

If the enemy springs his invasion stunt he is going to cause all the excitement he possibly can, for panic and fear and uncertainty and shaky bodies will help him tremendously. But if every individual fighter of all our forces aims with a cool aim then the enemy will simply be annihilated, no matter what his numbers.

This efficiency which comes through steadiness applies not only to the rifle shot, but to the machine gunner and bomb thrower also. Think a lot of what I've said about practising not to allow the mind to become excited, there's a very great deal in it.

After average eyesight and a steady body there is one more rule which the rifle shot should understand, then quietly cultivate. The knack of holding the breath perfectly for three seconds. It is the last thing you do just before and as you take the second pull, that tiny pressure which releases the trigger and sends the bullet on its way.

If you do not realize the reason why and then learn to hold the breath for three seconds while the body is utterly moveless then all the careful sighting, all the practice in the world will never make you a crack rifle shot. You will become a rifle shot certainly but never the marksman who nearly always gets his man.

The reason is simple. Your body is solid as a rock. Your

rifle sights are perfectly aligned on the target. You have taken the first pull even but—you are still breathing. Well, that faintest movement at the critical moment almost certainly will move the rifle muzzle but the merest fraction of an inch and—you miss the target.

A man's head at 300 yards is small enough, at 1000 it is small indeed. I've seen many a soldier miss a man in full view at 300 yards let alone a man's head at 1000, which is a general front line range. When your sights are aligned on a man's head at 1000 yards it takes but the merest wisp of movement of the rifle muzzle to cause the bullet to fly just wide of the mark.

If your body and grip is firm and moveless, if aim is correct, if you hold the breath at the moment of firing and all of you and the rifle are perfectly still, the bullet must fly to its mark.

Grasp the vital necessity of steadiness before you practise shooting, and you have laid the foundation to becoming a good shot. It only needs practice then and very soon you will consistently hit the bull at 1000 yards. And the extreme confidence which such good shooting will give you will mean that 1200 then 1500 yard shooting will become easy, while 500 yards, 200 yards (close range shooting) will become child's play.

CHAPTER III
The Firing Position:
Aiming

THE best training for an Auxiliary is, in my opinion, imm-
ediate practice in the things that count. That is the best
training for a regular army too, if I may have the cheek to
say so. Cut out the spit and polish, and get on with the job.
The first evening when issued with your rifle you will, or
should, learn its mechanism, loading, cleaning, care of the
weapon, etc. If your rifle instructors are practical men you'll
master all that in a couple of hours. The next evening you
should be out on the range and get in a couple of hours'
shooting before dark.

First make yourself comfortable, in the lying down position which is the position you'll generally do your fighting in.
Quickly realize that your rifle and Mother Earth will be your
two closest friends when the whips begin to crack. Hug
Mother Earth, for she'll save your life many a time, the tini-
est wrinkle in her vast face can save you from bullet and shell
if only you quickly learn how to take advantage of it.

As you make yourself comfortable facing the target (with
body lying a little left) rest your rifle on the ground, let
the ground take the weight as the weapon is loosely
clasped in the hands. Thus there is no strain on the sinews

and muscles of the arms while you are waiting to fire. When in action you'll remember to do the same thing, for this helps steadiness of rifle and body when the time comes to take aim.

Now, there is an actual firing position, a scientific position which has only been learned by an army of good shots throughout years of practice. Learn this position at the very first practice.

Don't face the target straight; that is, don't settle down with your head and body in a straight line with the distant target. Your body should lie a little left; that is, it lies easily and naturally a little to the left while your face can comfortably look straight towards the target. (A left handed shooter would lie in the position, his body inclined a little to the right.) Now, when you aim, your face is looking directly at the target. In this position the rifle butt rests solidly and immovably into the right shoulder with the muzzle pointing directly towards the bull. In slightly more "technical" terms, the body lies fairly oblique to the line of fire.

The legs are spread out, with the inside of the feet gripped firmly against, almost into, the ground. Wriggle about a bit for ease and comfort and firmness. If you can manage to jam part of your heels into the ground or hard down and against rock or timber you will feel that your knees and heels actually grip the ground. This position gives the body great firmness, allowing you absolute control of the rifle. The barrel does not shake or waver as it would were you in an uncomfortable, or incorrect position. The object is to make the body an immovable base glued firmly to the ground. The steadier your body the steadier your nerves and the more invisible you are, for one unguarded movement may betray you to the sniper seeking you. Hence, in every practice remember you are not only practising to shoot straight, you also are constantly practising to save your life.

Now raise the rifle. You find that chest, head, arms rise up as you prepare to aim.

This brings us to two very important points, both of which to you may often mean the difference between life and death. The first point is the position of the elbows, which brings us automatically to the second point, namely, the height you have raised your head above the ground. If your elbows have raised your forehead but a quarter of an inch higher than necessary, then that is just sufficient for a sniper's bullet.

Consider your arms and elbows as stays. You know that if you stay a baulk of timber you strengthen it considerably and make it perfectly solid and moveless. It is the connecting stays which do this. Well, your arms are stays acting in conjunction with your body and outspread legs to bring firmness and immobility to the rifle. All this is preparatory to the last final act, the utter immobility of the rifle as you fire.

Now, if you read any military textbook on the rifle you will see explicit instructions on the holding of the rifle. These are very good, and ours follow the rules very closely. But there is a very slight difference here and there, a slight elasticity from cast-iron textbook rules, as it were. And I believe this little difference will make you a better shot.

First, here's explaining why I reckon I'm competent to give you this advice. Since boyhood I've used a rifle. In manhood over periods I have used it to get a living, such as wallaby shooting, kangaroo shooting, crocodile shooting. For many wandering years I have depended mainly on the rifle for meat. Then, I've had very close on four years front line experience, with a lot of sniping experience thrown in. Have both sniped and been sniped at, very often. If I did not know what I was writing about I certainly would not now be here to tell the tale, I'd be bone dust on some Turkish sandhill. Hence, follow the textbooks by all means; those by recognized authorities are very good. But give a lot of thought to the hints here because they are bull's-eye hints.

When the rifle is lifted to aim the elbows are slightly spread; they, head and portion of the chest closely form a triangle. But, there are several kinds of triangles, the textbook triangle, and our more elastic one for instance. The textbook teaches to keep your left arm, your elbow, closely in under the rifle, always with the left wrist closely in under the rifle. Try it, and you almost certainly will feel a slight strain. Such a position will force you to bring in the right elbow closer to the body, which will mean a weakening of that "stay" effect. Also, and this seems to have been an entirely unnoticed effect, that very action forces you to raise your head an inch or two higher. When you hear hundreds of bullets whistling past your head you'll wish it was right into the ground.

Now as to position. Comfort above all things. If you feel comfort it means no part of you is under strain; you are master of the rifle. Assume the firing position but let the elbow spread out a little, just as much as is comfortable while giving you a firm grip on the rifle. Your left hand grips the rifle just so far forward as feels comfortable and firm. Settle the rifle butt firmly but comfortably into your shoulder, with the right hand grasp the small of the butt with the trigger finger round the trigger. The chin should now press comfortably down and against the butt.

This position will have brought your right elbow into alignment with the complete body, the rifle should feel as firm as if it were clasped in a vice, which is exactly what you are seeking. If you correctly manoeuvre your body so that it becomes a vice for the rifle then have no fear that you will never become a dead shot. No matter what your inexperience, physical disabilities, age, or even shakiness, once you grasp this mechanical knack of holding your rifle in a vice you must become a dead shot.

Rifle shooting is like everything else. To attain perfection you must think about it first, must understand the reasons why, and then go the right way to do it from the start. Just think a little about these simple hints, because if you master them it actually means that you have gone a long way to becoming a crack shot even before you have fired fifty shots. To the man who already is a medium shot these hints will explain the reasons why he is not a crack shot. Hence, a few more hints.

The secret of a crack shot is that he must make his body a solid vice, which he can only do by lying, or kneeling in a comfortable, solid, and controlled position. If then, he has trained his mind to take no notice of what is happening around him, he can drill an enemy's head clean through at a distance even of 1200 yards. At that distance the target would only appear as a little dot, but—it would be enough. While an enemy's body even at 2000 yards would be no longer safe.

If the rifleman learns the knack of settling his body in such a position (as described) that the weapon is held as in a vice then even if a man is a trifle unsteady of firing finger the bullet must hit its mark (the range being correct) for the simple fact that the rifle, once correctly sighted, cannot move. The firing finger in such a position acts independently of the body. Once the aim is taken in such a comfortable, vice-like grip, the aim *cannot* be disturbed.

The object of the rifleman is to attain this vice-like posture — comfortably. If he feels the least bit uncomfortable, if an elbow feels slightly uncomfortable, if a wrist feels the least strain, then he has not made of his body a 100 per cent vice.

Do not overdo it or you will create the very strain you seek to do away with. To show in another way what I mean just imagine you seize an enemy by the throat. Then every nerve, every sinew, every muscle, the mind, is at highest tension. That is not the grip at all. You settle the body as described and the rifle "automatically" comes to rest in a grip which is vice-like, but without serious strain. When in the military, I was ordered to fix myself in such a manner that should support the rifle. Whereas, in the bush, when dinner absolutely depended on hitting game at extreme range with the one shot, I used to settle down and make my rifle the last stay which firmly supported *me*.

Try and do this. The rifle is then part of you; it is absolutely immovable. If you have judged, and set your sights to, the correct range then your quarry is dead meat.

Remember, the barrel of a rifle is a round, straight tube. Should you hold the "body" of the rifle the faintest bit skew-whiff the barrel of course is then held out of line, the bullet will fly feet—yards—wide of the mark. The correct firing position prevents this. The comfortable "bed" for the butt in the shoulder, the immovable foundation of the body,

Now for the right hand. For a perfect grip this is firmly around the small of the butt so that the trigger finger is comfortably around the trigger, the thumb being over the small of the butt. The complete hand must grip the small of the rifle in such a way that the trigger finger can move without affecting the other fingers. Thus the right hand does its job of helping steady the rifle while the trigger finger is free to fire it; that finger's gently independent moving action does not affect the steadying hand at all. If your hand has to move in the slightest manner while the finger pulls the trigger then of course the barrel moves and the bullet flies wide. Once you settle the right hand in its grip that grip must not move, but the firing finger will be free to move quite freely.

Now realize the weight, and steadying power of your right cheek or right chin, against the butt. You can lower your head slightly to sight the rifle and this brings your chin and cheek down against the butt, yet again steadying it by downward pressure and also pressure against the shoulder. All these little points are what make of your body and the parts thereof the foundation, and the vice which hold the rifle immovable. The position, the body, the outspread legs, the knees, the "sides" of the feet, the elbows, arms, hands, right shoulder, cheek, all have their separate jobs which combine into one to hold your rifle absolutely immovable. And the mastery of that position is the secret of the crack shot.

Now we come to aiming. This, like every other action of rifle shooting must first be understood to be done properly. Once understood you cannot miss.

To aim, first realize the necessity for aligning your sights the same way shot after shot. It is useless aiming with a full sight one shot, a low sight next shot, and variations during the next. You would be surprised how many men do this, simply because they do not know how to aim in the first place. They hit the target all over the place, miss it altogether, occasionally fluke a bull's-eye. And wonder why.

Such erratic shooting is often caused by taking a varying degree of sight with different shots. Learn to sight correctly, then always stick to the same sight.

Remember this: Possibly you may have some little peculiarity of sight, or some freaky twist of body that makes the correct sight not correct to you.

Never mind. If convinced by actual practice that this is so, then experiment. So long as you can hold your rifle immovable then there is a correct sight for you. It may be more or much less of the foresight. It may be some slightly differing manipulation of the sight. I've even known a few excellent shots who could not shoot straight unless by a slight canting of the barrel, which would mean failure to 97 per cent other men. Never mind, find out just what your little peculiarity is, either in firing position or aiming. Then, once you find your individual aim which strikes the bull, stick to it. Memorize it firmly. Always use that one aim.

And now we'll get back to the aiming which suits 95 per cent, and more, of shooters. The backsight of a service rifle in general is of the U type that of the sporting a V. For the service rifle you take a full sight.

This means that through the U (backsight) you take in all the blade of the foresight until the tip is in perfectly straight line with the shoulders of the backsight. If using a sporting rifle and taking a fine sight then only the very tip of the foresight would be visible right down in the bottom of the V. But we will stick to the service rifle for that is what you should be issued with.

Imagine you are about to aim. You shall set your sights to the exact range, 1000 yards. Your target is the head of an enemy peering up over a ridge.

The fool has forgotten all about the skyline so that his turnipy-looking head is silhouetted. You keep your eyes on him while breathing normally, steadily raising the rifle. When you judge the muzzle is "two feet below" him close the left eye and calmly sight, steadily bringing up the rifle muzzle. First, focus your eye on the foresight automatically bringing up the muzzle until the foresight blade appears full length perfectly upright in centre of the U, until you almost or very faintly see the platform of the foresight block in the bottom of it. Breathe a little slower and deeper now as the rifle muzzle slowly comes up in perfect line just below the man's head. Take a slow, deep breath, and hold it. The next faintest, upward movement of the rifle and the bottom of the man's chin is perfectly balanced upon the blade of the foresight as your trigger finger softly takes the first pull. Just a fraction of a second of utter steadiness, then—let him have it.

CHAPTER IV
Aiming: Firing

IF you are a Regular, instructors will teach you; if an Irregular then when you get out on the range old hands will show you the firing position in a moment. Try it out, then apply for yourself the hints I've given. If the position you've been shown proves uncomfortable, you know it's not quite right.

Remember what has been written here (it is simple and easy to remember) then wriggle about until you become thoroughly "set" as explained in the last chapter. If you apply the hints in that chapter to yourself and your rifle, then in eighty cases out of a hundred you will soon become a better shot than your instructor, probably a much better shot. Now a little about rifle sights—just those few necessary little points you should know about them to help you shoot straight.

The main part of a military foresight is the blade, the top of which is called the tip. It is this blade which counts. The blade is set perfectly upright in a foresight block, like an inverted T, thus $\perp$. All of that straight blade must be focused on the target which means in practice that the bottom centre of the target is "balanced" upon the tip of the foresight thus:

The blade is embedded in the foresight block, appearing as it were like an upright needle set into a little flat platform of steel. When the surface of this platform appears it is a warning to your eye not to go below it. So that, when aiming, bring in all the foresight blade from tip to bottom until the flat line of block upon which it rests just almost comes into view. Jutting out well away from and up above the foresight are two metal leaves, really a sight protector. A new hand with a military rifle is sometimes liable to mistake one of these leaves for the foresight, in which case of course his shot goes "miles" wide of the mark. Memorize these leaves, this sight protector, and you will never make the same mistake.

The back or rearsight contains the U, through which you focus the blade of the foresight. The blade, when correctly aimed, fits dead centre down this U from top to bottom. As a guide to warn you against raising the foresight too high there is the block of the foresight which would come into view. Also the shoulders of the backsight. These also warn you against taking too little of the foresight. The shoulders of the backsight are the top line of metal from which the U is cut. These shoulders go straight out from each upper edge of the U. If your foresight is in perfect alignment then if a hair were stretched across the U the tip of the foresight and shoulders of the U would make a perfectly straight line.

This rearsight also controls the elevation, the range. It is graduated into yards, set at from 200 for point-blank range then from 300 yards onward to extreme range. The movable slide upon this rear-sight raises or lowers the sight to the elevation, that is, the range estimated. An instructor or rifle shooting comrade will explain such particulars to you, in a lecture or a few minutes' talk.

It has been explained to you how to aim at a man's head at 1000 yards. So that you may thoroughly grasp what you must do with your sights, we'll aim now at a target, a regulation bull's-eye at 1000 yards.

Carry on exactly as already described. But, before you fire, let us see if you thoroughly understand "balancing the bull".

You "balanced" the man's head on the tip of your foresight; "held" the bottom centre of his chin exactly balanced upon the foresight tip of which was in exact line with the shoulders of the U. The bullet would take that unwary enemy fair between the eyes.

Balance the round, black disc of the bull's-eye similarly, but leave under it the faintest white line, just as if the centre of the bottom of the black dot were balanced upon the faintest line of air resting upon the tip of the foresight.

Thus you have hit the bull's-eye. Having got the above firmly in your mind's eye, here are a few points to understand and memorize so that you will become a consistent crack shot.

You understand and have mastered the firing position which makes of the rifle a weapon gripped in a controlled but unstrained vice. You understand the few vital principles of aiming. Now, your firing position being accurate and comfortable ensures that your body does not become strained or tired. But your eye is a more delicate organization and, unless it is used as understandingly as your body, it may strain or tire, which means that the sights or target blurs, may even waver.

Hence, understand the job your eye must do in relation to the sights and target.

The eye focuses the sights upon the target. Now, there are two sights and the target, three in all. This is a job for three focusing actions and in doing all three you take longer to aim and the eye is liable to strain a little, to grow weary.

Personally, I have, since a boy, concentrated immediately on the foresight then just at the right time the target and back-sight come into focus almost automatically, as of themselves. The military advise to focus on the target first. I tried it, but didn't shoot nearly so well. So I advise you to train your eye by immediately picking out the foresight first.

When coming up to the aim start the rifle muzzle just below the target as described. As you raise it your eye immediately picks out the foresight, the tip of which as the rifle is gently raised immediately comes under the centre bottom of the bull's-eye, then the blade of the foresight comes into the U and the bull's-eye is "balanced".

Tip of foresight under bottom centre of target; blade of foresight perfectly upright in centre of U; tip of foresight in perfect line with shoulders of U.

To aim any other way not only takes longer, but is an added strain to the eye.

When the bull is balanced upon the foresight blade the tip, as described, is in dead line with the shoulders of the U. If you are a slow aimer this hair line adjustment of the eye and sights and target is so fine that you may become momentarily confused as to whether it exactly is in line, and whether it may not be a shade too low. I always beat this confusion by allowing the extreme tip of the sight to just show above the U, that is a shade higher than the level of the U shoulders. The tip only just breaks that delicate imaginary hair line and is instantly noticeable. Thus uncertainty or hesitation is immediately done away with.

Fire instantly when certain the bull's-eye is yours. Never take longer to aim than necessary because the longer you take the more likely that sights or target will become blurred or wavery. If your firing position is correct you'll have sufficient time to take deadly aim without overdoing, straining, and spoiling it. This is the reason I advise bringing up the rifle from below the target. As your rifle muzzle rises it does so immediately below the bottom centre of the target, and practically immediately is right on the target and you are focusing sights and target. There is no waste time; your eye has a good chance of doing its job without strain or uneasiness; the arms have no time to feel strain.

The method I've just explained makes it very easy for the eye, exactly as the slow upward movement of the rifle straight to the mark makes it dead easy for the hands and body. Otherwise, so far as your eye is concerned it would be glancing at the distant target then back to the foresight and back to the rear-sight and back to the target all over again. That is what many a rifle shot does, then gives up in despair declaring his eyes must be "bad". Nothing of the sort. He does not understand the job that his body, his rifle sights, and eye have to do—that is all. In those few critical moments he strains his eye, gives it half a dozen things to do over and over again until it becomes watery, or target and sights blur, and arms begin to twitch. A man can shoot deadly with left or right eye, with spectacles, with both eyes open for the matter of that, if he understands the job. The crack shot becomes a crack shot when he understands what his body and rifle sights and eye have to do.

Immediately you make a good shot you will be pleased. Memorize exactly your feelings as you held the rifle, everything you did, how the sights and target appeared. It is surprising what a mental picture can be formed, and left firmly implanted upon the mind. Afterwards, the subconscious mind (call it what you like) seeks to help you attain exactly the same result again, if you care to call upon it. Do so, and you will shoot well again.

I have mentioned that deep breath, and the holding of it just before you press the trigger. This gives to the body at the critical moment, an utter movelessness. It means that, if you have held the rifle correctly, if your range and sighting is correct, nothing can stop that bullet hitting the bull fair and square.

Should you mess the business up, feel you are not exactly on the target, then lower the rifle, take a breath or two, switch the eyes aside to glance at something else a moment, then concentrate and aim again. If the target is a living one he has to wait for you of course. But if you are well concealed he will not know you are "drawing a bead on him". If you fire and miss he certainly will know and will probably disappear. After which it will be you or he for it. Remember that last deep breath, and to hold it, just before you press the trigger.

One more point to remember—trigger pressing. This is important. But if you have grasped the reason for the method in holding the rifle, trigger pressing will come automatically, for your hand and finger will be exactly in the right position.

The thumb and three fingers of the right hand are already gripping the small of the butt, with the trigger finger loosely around the trigger. Now remember! That trigger finger has quite a different job to do than the remainder of the hand. The grip of the hand is firm but not tight as the rifle muzzle rises to the aim. As the foresight engages the target then the grip of the body, the firmness of legs and feet, the holding pressure of the chin, the grip of left and right hand then become stronger. But the trigger finger still remains at ease. As the target balances over the foresight then rear-sight, and the deep holding breath is taken, the trigger finger steadily presses in the first pull. One last split second of utter stillness and certainty then the. trigger finger steadily squeezes and the shot is off.

Those are the movements as clearly explained as I am able. Understand them, follow them out in practice, and you are a crack shot.

Here are a few reasons why, in pulling the trigger, many a man is not a crack shot. At the critical moment he jerks the trigger. This immediately jerks the muzzle slightly upward and the shot misses.

He clenches his finger too tightly around the trigger before he is ready to fire. The finger cannot then, on its own initiative as it were, respond with a light touch when the nerves signal it "pull".

He has not got his right hand gripping correctly. To press the trigger he finds he has slightly to move his right hand, and this in turn slightly moves the direction of the muzzle. He starts too soon to urge his finger to get ready to pull or squeeze the trigger and in doing so probably tires his eye and makes his finger "nervous".

When he has taken and holds that last deep breath, his right hand is not then grasping the small of the butt as firmly as it should. Then, when the finger does press, the slackness of his right grip allows the barrel to waver just a shade.

He dawdles too long. Has taken the first pull and the target is perfectly balanced, but still he dawdles. And he who hesitates when all is set, is lost.

Note that the trigger of a service rifle has two actions: one is the "first pull", the second is the fire. The main idea is that a recruit won't "pull off his shot" too soon. The first pull is a warning "ready", a "steadier" as it were. Just a little pull, and the trigger clicks ready for the firing pull.

With most sporting rifles there is only one pull, a touch mostly. To a rifle that is set very fine one touch on the trigger means that the weapon goes off.

Whatever you do in rifle fire, unless sudden close action rushes upon you and you must whip up your rifle and fire, don't hurry your shot. At the same time memorize the necessity for getting perfect aim as quickly as possible, then fire instantly when you do. Otherwise, not only may the target move, but if you dally your rifle may begin to waver, your sights or target blur.

Most men, especially when firing under certain atmospheric conditions and are anxious to shoot, find their target or sights going "blurry". The only remedy is to forget about it and the blur will evaporate like a mirage. It generally means that anxiety is straining your eyes, actually making them "nervous". And the last thing you want in rifle shooting is anxiety. Forget it.

Here is something to doubly reassure you. If the target blurs a bit, it doesn't matter much so long as your sights also have not blurred. And they won't blur so long as you focus the foresight first, then fire immediately your aim is set.

As explained, bring up the foresight straight away to balance the bottom centre of the target. Carry on just as described and it doesn't matter if the target does blur because your sights are already dead set upon it. Understand?

Remember, at the moment of firing, that tight but not straining grip with the right hand. It is this grip which allows the trigger finger to do its particular job without tautness or jerk. If your right hand grip is in a correct and comfortable position while gripping firmly then the only job the trigger finger can do is pull the trigger. But if your right grip is loose or in an uncomfortable grasp then at the critical moment the trigger finger cannot operate comfortably and independently and messes up the job.

CHAPTER V
Judging Distances

You now have a thorough foundation for being a crack shot under normal conditions; nothing can stop you if you have understood the previous chapters.

We will now imagine that you are out on your own, an enemy may appear at any moment and you must fire at him in the open countryside with only your own skill and knowledge to help you. Well, he cautiously appears, away over that distant rise. He comes into view like a little wallaby sneaking through the grass. He disappears. You hide, seeking a safe and comfortable cover position that will command all the ground possible between you and the rise. You know that sooner or later he must worm his way over the rise, or around it, or along one of the little gullies running from the side or below the rise.

You immediately estimate the distance of that rise, get the range. Unless you estimate the range closely you cannot hit the enemy no matter how. carefully you shoot. To become a good judge of distance is like everything else, you must first understand the subject, and know why you must understand it.

The trajectory, otherwise the line of flight of a bullet, is not in a straight line. It leaves the rifle muzzle and travels in a "curved" flight, the farther the object the higher the bullet rises until it gradually and evenly falls on to the mark. To gain this elevation is the reason of the graduated back sights. It allows the slide on the rear sight to be raised according to the estimation of the range. Hence the rifle-man when aiming is raising the muzzle of the rifle while at the same time he can still see, and sight at the target. The muzzle being raised gives elevation to the bullet, the correct elevation if the sight has been raised to the correct range. And now the bullet, if the rifle is correctly sighted, will hit its mark. So that the judging of distance is a matter of elevation and is of extreme importance. If you do not judge your distance correctly then the "elevation" of the bullet will carry it either short of or beyond the target, depending whether you have set your sights too high, or too low.

It is a simple matter on the rifle range for the targets are spaced at from 200 yards, 300 yards to a 1000 and beyond. You simply set your rear sight at 500 yards if firing at a 500 yard range, and so on. But when away from the range there is nothing to guide you, except what you have learned.

Hence, your instructors at the range should teach you not only rifle shooting but what is vitally important as well—judging range or distance.

As is often the case, once you get the idea your best instructor will be yourself. At every opportunity memorize the distance between the ranges. Turn your head away and sight some object that you estimate to be the same distance. Turn back to the range again and see whether you have over or under estimated.

When the range is not in actual use you should step out

the different ranges, then by the eye memorize the distances. Three hundred yards, 500, 700 and so on. Then send a man away out from the range to stand at 200 yards up to 1200. Memorize the distance between him and you at various ranges, fix each distance as firmly as possible in your mind, remember that when in action you will not have a large, evenly spaced target in front of you. Your target will be indistinct and probably with all manner of broken ground between you and it, and only by your own experience will you be able to estimate the distance between you and it.

Your instructor should also point out to you the apparent size of a man standing, kneeling, and lying at 500 yards, at 1000, at 1500. Try to memorize the appearance of a figure at varying distances; it will be found very helpful. A man "grows smaller" with every 100 yards he is away from you. Clench your hand, with the first and second fingers outspread (just like a V sight). Hold your hand straight out in front then sight the man between the arms of the V. Memorize his size thus at each range. There are a number of different methods which help you to judge distance; study each one suggested and memorize any part of any system which you feel will help you. Get a good idea of ranges up to 400 yards, a little practice will soon make you familiar with them. Later, success in estimating farther ranges will depend almost entirely on the training you give your own judgment, and on memorizing. For instance, if you can judge distances accurately up to 300 yards, then you have memorized those distances firmly.

Your target is now out in the open at a much farther range. Well, sight the distance to what you are certain is 300 yards. By eyesight mark a stone, a tree, anything that happens to be exactly where you consider that 300 yards is. Then glance from there to the target. Is it 300 yards farther? Yes. Well, from the spot you've "marked" try to estimate 300 yards farther on. "Mark" that spot. Then estimate how many hundred yards the object is from the second spot. Probably you will get quite close to the range. Certainly so with practice. Thus fix 100 yards, 200, 300, right up to 1000 yards, if you can, firmly in your mind. Many men can do so with practice. And when you are memorizing these ranges do so not only in the lying down firing position, but when standing up and when kneeling. Compare each set of results with the other sets. Because if solid war comes here you will be called upon to fire in all three positions, just according to circumstances. On the great majority of occasions you will fire from the lying down position.

Study every method of "fixing" different ranges, for each helps in some detail to indelibly imprint distances on your mind. Keep remembering that, when the whips are cracking, if you cannot accurately estimate your own range you cannot get your man. And you may be out on your own, with no one near to help you if you miss.

A good guide, always, is the appearance of a man at certain distances. At 200 yards all details of him are clearly visible. At 300 yards his face is blurred. At 400 yards his body appears pretty well as usual but it is difficult to distinguish his face. At 500 yards you can still see his limbs though not too clearly while his body seems to have "thinned down" from the shoulders. At 600 yards his head is only a dot; he doesn't seem to have any limbs, and he's grown very thin.

Points like those you instructors will explain to you, and it is up to you to memorize them. One method is by the blade of the foresight. Imagine a man kneeling to take a pot shot at you between 200 and 300 yards. You'd let him have it quickly of course because you'd guess that distance easily. But if you aimed at him so that the blade of the foresight was just beside him, he would appear to be kneeling on the bed of the foresight and his head would be on a level with the tip of the foresight. His range would be about midway between 200 and 300 yards. If a man were standing at 400 yards he would be just the height of the blade of the foresight. Train the foresight right beside him and you would see him standing by the blade and just the same height as it. His range would then be 400 yards. If he were an actual enemy you would slip your back-sight up to 400 yards then balance his belt buckle on the tip of your foresight and—he'd be dead meat.

Once you've got 200 or 300 or even 1000 yards, firmly fixed in your mind, then when going to work estimate the distance between the telegraph poles. Then step them out and see exactly what they do measure. Day after day memorize that distance, memorize it until you've got the distance between quite a number of poles. The same with electric light standards and other objects. When a man is coming towards you down the street or elsewhere estimate his distance, his range. Then instantly mark a spot; he may be passing a gate or a pillar box. As you walk along step out the distance to it and see if your judgment of range is correct. Each fairly long step is approximately a yard. A reliable rule is that 120 paces measure approximately 100 yards.

After your section or platoon (if you are in charge of one) have had a bit of practice, when "outside" send a man to stand up, kneel, and lie down at any distance you like. Ask each man to judge the distance. If the range is a long one and the country helps to make him distinct one method of finding an approximate range is this way: "Is he 800 yards distant?" "I'm sure he's at least that; I wouldn't be surprised if he's a lot more." Then ask "Is he 1200 yards away?" "No. . . . He may be just that, but I doubt it. He certainly isn't a shade farther than 1200 yards." Very well, then. You're certain he is at least 800 yards away. You're certain he is not a shade more than 1200 yards away. So halve the difference, and 1000 yards is your estimate of his range.

Try that way up to a mile. It's surprising how quickly you will become an accurate judge of distance—which is range. You can of course find your own range by a couple of trial shots. But that would not do if you were ambushing a man, or stalking him, for it would immediately warn him and perhaps put your position away. If such considerations did not apply, you could put up the sights, then fire at a dry patch of ground near the target. Then move your sight higher or lower according to the spurt of dust. If the dust showed that the bullet fell short then put the sight to a longer range, and vice versa.

We started this chapter with waiting for an enemy who has momentarily shown himself above a rise 1000 yards to a mile away. You were measuring the range to that rise, and you've got it, for by now you should be a good judge of distance as well as a good rifle shot. So that the confidence is yours. But because this is a matter of life and death.

On a bright, cloudless day a man may appear to be closer than he actually is. He appears closer if the marksman is looking at him across a valley. This can happen too if the target is on a plain and a bright sun is behind the marksman. The target may also look closer if standing on the other side of a river or lake on a bright day.

In drizzly, cloudy, or misty weather, a man may appear to be farther away that he actually is. If he is standing or crouching in shade he appears farther away. If he has a dark background behind him, such as a shadowed hill, he may appear to be farther away. Even if you are looking at him across a maze of gullies, he generally appears further away than he actually is. If you are in heavily timbered country a distant man appears to be farther away than he actually is. So much for distance.

Now for wind. Because a strong wind has the power of blowing a bullet wide of its course—depending on the strength of the wind, the direction, and the distance the bullet has to travel. So that when shooting on a windy day some allowance must be made for wind; the shorter the range the less allowance of course.

First, be sure of the direction of the wind. You can feel it on your face maybe. Can see a wisp of smoke or dust, which shows the way the wind is blowing. Watch the trees or grass near the target. Make up your mind also whether the wind is steady, or gusty. If gusty, the wind may drop before you fire with the result that if you've allowed for wind you'll miss the target.

If the wind is blowing across your rifle barrel you make an allowance by aiming a little to the right or left, according to the direction and strength of the wind, and the distance of the target. The farther the target the greater the influence of the wind upon the bullet.

Two things, particularly, must be remembered: (a) do not get "windy"; (b) remember elevation.

By windy I mean do not imagine there is a wind, or that the wind is stronger than it is. Some marksmen are liable to become "wind-conscious" when there is hardly any wind at all. Perhaps this is because they frequently hear their fellow marksmen discussing wind.

If there is a strong wind blowing, then don't forget elevation, and take a full sight. You will be making some allowance, that is, aiming a little to right or left of the target. As, now, you will not be balancing the target or the sights you are very liable to aim too low, to take in too little of the foresight blade and thus lose elevation, lose range. That is a common fault when aiming "off" the target, an easily understood oversight when not aiming directly at the target. A target, a bull's-eye or man as the case may be is a perfect guide for the sights; you balance the target on the tip and take in through the U all the blade of the foresight. But when you are firing to left or right of a target it is "not there" to balance on the sight. The common experience then is that the marksman takes in too little of the foresight and his bullet falls short. Be sure then, to take in a very full foresight, even though it may appear to be just a little too much.

CHAPTER VI
Allowing for Wind

A SIDE wind, a wind blowing from your left or right will need more allowance than a head wind, one blowing from the target towards you, or a rear wind, one blowing from behind you to the target. These head and rear winds need not bother you much. If a very strong head wind is blowing, aim normally at the target but use a shade more elevation; instead of balancing the bottom of the bull on the foresight lift the tip of the foresight an "inch" up into the bull. If a very strong rear wind is blowing, use a shade less elevation.

Then there is the right-angle wind. Like the cross wind and side wind, it comes from your right or left. Then there is the oblique wind. The diagram explains.

A wind may be very mild and not make much difference. As a rule a "fresh breeze" is a wind that may be blowing at about ten miles per hour; a "strong wind" is one that blows at about twenty miles per hour. On these figures a table of wind allowance has been worked out which is a reasonable guide. You must judge the wind strength for yourself. What we will call a fresh breeze is one that will blow your hat off if you don't jam it tight on your head. This is a ten-mile-an-hour

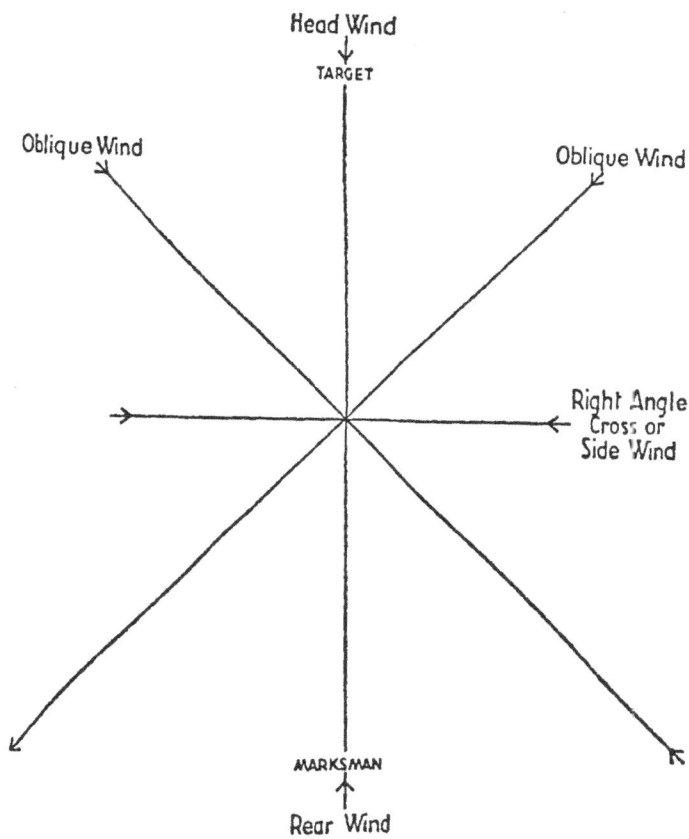

Head Wind

TARGET

Oblique Wind

Oblique Wind

Right Angle
Cross or
Side Wind

MARKSMAN

Rear Wind

breeze. A twenty miler is one you've got to bow to if you walk against it. These two breezes are the standard and it is again-st these that the following table, up to a range of 600 yards has been compiled.

If an oblique wind happens to be blowing (see diagram) then halve those figures for the allowance. The reason is that the oblique wind is blowing at such an angle that its strength can only carry the bullet half way out of its course, as comp-ared with a side wind.

Say you are shooting on a windy day and you reckon the wind (a side wind from the right) is blowing at a good ten miles per hour. Your range is 500 yards and you are aiming two feet to the right of the target, that two feet right being the wind allowance. The wind presently increases to twenty miles per hour. You then double the wind allowance which brings the sights four feet to the right of the target. And so on. If the wind wanes in strength, lessen your allowance acc-ording to what you estimate its lessened strength.

Fresh breeze blowing at about ten miles per hour:

Range: 200	300	400	500	600
Allow: 6in.	1ft.	1ft.6in.	2ft.	2ft.6in.

Strong wind blowing at twenty miles per hour:

Range: 200	300	400	500	600
Allow: 1ft.	2ft.	3ft.	4ft.	5ft.

You know how uncertain winds are; how they often die down, then blow up again; how they may suddenly shift to another quarter and as suddenly blow back again, only to die down or veer off in some other direction. On a very windy day watch out for variations of direction together with increasing or decreasing strengths of wind, for if you can estimate these correctly you are going to hit the bull's-eye. If you are in action, you are going to hit your man. And he, not knowing or not understanding the varying effects of winds upon a bullet, or being too eager or excited to take the matter into consideration, is going to miss you. When you've got him, you get his mate too which saves the life of your mate. And so it goes on. The cool, thoughtful rifle shot is the one who hits his man while the poor shot is the one who gets hit and also wastes his "ton of lead".

But don't let a windy day bother you; windy days must come and go. Be patient if you find your shots missing in action; you can be quite sure the other fellow is missing too. Watch the effect of each shot; the tell-tale spurt of dust is the very best guide you can have. If the bullet clips the dust a foot to the right of his head then you instantly know you must aim a foot nearer 'left next time, and you've got him.

Whether on the target or in action on a decidedly windy day remember that no man can definitely and consistently judge the variations of a wind and its certain effect upon a bullet. Even the best men can but make allowances which they estimate from their own knowledge, thought, experience —and above all by the effect of their shots. If you are firing under conditions which show you the effect of your shots, that is the best guide of all; you instantly see the allowance to be made for your next shot.

Throughout many years of shooting under peace-time and active service conditions a windy day bothered me very little, once I'd learned that varying strengths and directions of wind had their own definite effect upon a bullet. Experience soon taught the allowance necessary at varying ranges. Every man must learn from his own particular experience, which thus trains his own personal judgment. The great advantage you now have is that you already know of these things; whereas many of us had to find out for ourselves.

There is a mechanical aid for shooting on a windy day, a small attachment called the wind gauge. It is fairly accurate at a stationary target under favourable conditions; even so, you must have experience first to manipulate it. It is extremely unlikely that your rifle will have a wind gauge attachment. I never ever saw one in four years of active service, nor in civil life except at a rifle club meet. Hence, I will not describe it here. After all, what you will have to depend upon is your rifle and, above all, what you carry in your head.

The military teach a system of aiming off against wind which I'll describe: Imagine a wind is blowing from the right. The object then is to aim, balance the target, then carefully move the muzzle slowly right, bringing the bull along the left shoulder of the back sight, probably to balance it on the extreme tip of the left shoulder. This ensures that at least you keep the elevation for you still see the bull's-eye, either resting on the right shoulder of the back sight or the left, according to which direction the wind is blowing. According to the varying ranges, and strength of wind the sights are "carried" farther to left or right upon the target itself.

Speaking personally, it is a difficult job, for one must

remember too many things at once. I believe your personal judgment, as previously explained, will prove the more accurate. Anyway, most of your targets will be men.

The military also teach a system of aiming off for wind with figure targets, which give a good approximate idea of wind allowance. Imagine your target is a standing man at between 300 and 400 yards. Your aim would be the buckle of his belt. But a fresh wind is blowing from the right say. Now imagine another man standing shoulder to shoulder with the target man, at the target man's left shoulder. Your aim then would be the belt buckle of the imaginary man. If the distance were 500 yards, you would imagine two men standing beside the target, and aim for the middle of the furthest.

Unfortunately, in action, your target will not always be stationary—not by a long way. It will be men crawling, creeping, walking, crouching, running, running steadily, running for all they're worth; it will be heads of men in cars or armoured cars, motor cyclists moving at different speeds under varying conditions along roads and across country. The slits and peep-holes in tanks, the parachutist, and the aeroplane will be targets. Imagine the difference in speed of these last two: the parachutist drifting down on the slant depending for speed on the air currents and strength of wind and agility in his manipulating the control cords of his chute, and the aeroplane coming and going at speeds of from 300 to 400 miles per hour.

Here there is another problem for you, a problem in movement, in varying speeds of moving targets; from the slow walk of an unwary man to the screaming 400 miles per hour dive of the aeroplane troop buster. How will you aim to hit each and all of these?

What a problem! But it is these problems that make rifle shooting fascinating. Quickly you will learn there is far more in it than simply putting a bullet in a gun and taking a pot shot. And, modem methods of war have complicated it all. But, instead of making the rifle and even the machine gun obsolete, this crazy speed has made them far more valuable weapons—to those who understand them, and to those Heads who understand their value.

For here is a secret. With all their speed, with all their 80-miles-per-hour motor cyclists, with all their 40-miles-per-hour tanks, with all their 500- miles-per-hour aeroplanes, these super speedsters cannot reach the speed of a rifle bullet. Not by a long, long way.

Hence, you still have 'em; your little ounce of lead can even stop a plane. Of course you must not only be a crack shot, but a crack judge of distances and speeds as well, to do it.

You begin to understand now how even regular armies use up a ton of lead to kill a man; to understand also how a body of riflemen, if only given expert instruction and plenty of practice with live ammunition under service conditions, would quickly become a terrible fighting force. One such regiment, fully trained in the use of the rifle could, arms being equal, defeat twenty times their number of ordinarily trained men.

You realize now that your rifle is a weapon that can do a big job indeed for you and your country, if only you understand it and know how to use it.

On a moderately clear day a man's head peering over a ridge 1000 yards away is dead meat to the crack shot. And yet that target is very small, a vague dot almost. How much larger then is a standing man at 1000 yards. And you do not have to balance his unseen chin on the tip of your foresight, you merely have to balance his belt buckle. This gives you a lot to come and go on. If your bullet is low you can still get him, if the bullet flies high you still get him. If you have not the exact range and incline to the idea that the range is nearer 100 than 1000 yards you merely aim anywhere from six inches to a foot above his belt and you still get him.

Even so, you will be surprised at the great number of men who would miss him. Many of us were fired at many and many times by rifles and machine guns throughout four years in the front line and yet we came home to tell the tale. In most of the fighting in which my regiment was engaged, we were right out in the open, too. So that there are hundreds of thousands of rotten bad shots in the trained armies of the world. Learn to shoot straight and your regiment of Irregulars will knock spots out of any allegedly trained enemy battalion.

The velocity of a bullet from a rifle muzzle varies with the type of rifle and ammunition used. We'll take an approximate speed with a service rifle using Mark VII ammunition. The muzzle velocity, that is, the speed with which the bullet leaves the rifle is at about 2500 feet per second. But it does not continue so. The bullet travels 600 yards the first second, 400 yards the next second, 300 yards the following second and thus decreases in speed with each second. Thus it takes two seconds to travel 1000 yards, between five and six seconds to travel one mile.

An aeroplane travelling at 400 miles per hour takes six seconds to travel 1173 yards. A bullet does 1760 yards (1 mile) in less than the same time.

We'll stick to 1000 yards; it is a good fighting range. A bullet takes two seconds to travel 1000 yards. A slowly walking man would take at least one step in that time, probably one and a bit. Hence he would travel at least three feet. If we had taken a stationary aim at him and made a perfect shot we'd miss by at least three feet.

He'd jump three feet. You'd get your laugh, but believe me not a second shot. He'd be down behind cover and looking for you with a nasty glint in his eye.

CHAPTER VII
Shooting at Moving Objects: Night Shooting

SO allowances must be made for moving targets, according to the range and speed with which the target is moving. You would allow more for a quickly walking man than a slowly walking one, considerably more for a running man. Allow still more for a trotting horse than a walking horse, more again for a cantering horse, considerably more for a galloping horse. The same principle applies to the speed of a motor cyclist or armoured car, or tank. And, of course, to the aeroplane.

In potting a moving target (unless travelling directly toward or away from you) you aim ahead of the target so that it will actually "run into" the bullet. It sounds difficult but, as with most difficulties, it only requires a little thought and experience to do it. I've known lots of self-taught bushmen who, with a 22 rifle, can hit a crow or hawk on the wing almost every time. Such men will seldom fire at a sitting shot; it is beneath their dignity. It was their own thought, observation, and practice that taught them such difficult shooting.

To be a crack shot at a moving target is to be an ace rifleman. Bush shooting first taught me the art. Years later I found that exactly the same principles apply to active service conditions. If you grasp the idea, which really is simple, you can teach yourself. Firstly, there is no need to bother should an enemy be walking straight towards or straight away from you. Just estimate the correct range, aim straight at him, and he's your man. But if he's walking across your front, you aim ahead of him of course. Say he is at 1000 yards range on an ordinary, non-windy day. A bullet will take two seconds to reach him. He will almost certainly take just two steps in that time but his body will only advance one yard, three feet. Well, you aim at an imaginary belt buckle, or slightly higher, just three feet ahead of him but keep the muzzle very, very faintly moving with him, then fire. And he walks into the bullet.

Now, he does not know you are there. If he did suspect your distant presence then he'd be an idiot to walk exposed like that, or else he'd be a brave man seeking to draw your fire. If you were a poor or ordinary shot he would be perfectly safe, but if you understood firing at a moving target then he'd be a dead hero.

Imagine aiming at this man. There's plenty of time. He's just walking along. Estimate his speed correctly, whether he's walking a shade faster than an ordinarily walking man, whether he has long legs that are taking slightly longer paces than we stumpy blokes take. If so, you must allow another six inches. You must estimate his speed correctly, the distance his body advances forward every two seconds.

Here is a really good method: Aim three feet ahead of him, then hold your rifle perfectly steady and count. One—two. If by then he's walked six inches past your stationary rifle muzzle you know you would have missed him. Try again, aiming three feet six inches or four feet ahead of him this time. If your sights cover him perfectly at the end of two, you know exactly the distance ahead of him to aim. Get it?

When you have taken your aim don't forget move ahead with the rifle as you fire.

That same rule applies to any moving target, but, of course, you must know your range in the first place. As a bullet takes a little more than five seconds to travel a mile then when aiming at a walking man a mile away you must aim feet further ahead of him than you would if he were only 1000 yards away. Then again, as a swiftly moving horse or car travels faster than a running man you must remember that in this case the target will soon travel, 100 yards and you must manipulate your sights accordingly. But the principle is the same, for all that. Bushmen shoot crows and hawks on the wing. They see the line of flight; they aim ahead according to range and wind (if any) and the varying speed of hawk or crow— and the target runs into the bullet.

So does an aeroplane, if it be flying low enough and the men below understand the speed of planes in accordance with the speed of their bullets. Many a battalion of 1000 rifles would have brought down many a plane in this war if they had only been trained to those simple facts.

You by now should have learned a lot about your rifle and what its sights, bullet, and you can do. Test yourself out! If you have compared these movements and distances and aiming points you will have realized that the secret of success is contained in that simple advice to: aim forward of the moving object; hold the rifle stationary; count the seconds until the object reaches your foresight. This gives you the distance to aim ahead providing you have the range correctly.

Knowing the range you know how long it will take the bullet to travel that distance.

Every individual man can thus train himself to accurately aim at a moving target. I say train because there is no rule of thumb in this secret. One man's second may be slightly faster or slower than another man's. His individual eyesight, and method of moving his rifle muzzle which is slowly moving along ahead of the target, will also be slightly different. So that each man, once he grasps the idea trains himself according to his own physical characteristics. The result is far more satisfactory than a copy book training could be.

So far as shooting at aeroplanes is concerned this present war on all fronts has proved that, under favourable circumstances, a trained body of riflemen, or a single good machine gunner has proved dangerous to aeroplanes. Just occasionally a plane has been brought down. But the main benefit is that the pilot above does not relish concentrated rifle and machine-gun fire, it may affect his nerve a bit which is not good for his aim. He may not come back for more. If he does he probably will fly higher. Whether or no there is a very good chance that his plane may be laid up back in the drome for repairs. Increasingly now we should be manufacturing armour-piercing bullets with which small arm fire against low-flying planes will become much more deadly.

By favourable conditions, I mean in the main, range. A man comes within range of a modern rifle at 2000 yards, although he can be hit at 2500 yards; with some brands of high power ammunition even at 3000 yards. But, from a single direct shot he is only in extreme peril at say 1500 yards, possibly a mile (1760 yards). Any closer than 1500 yards and he is dead meat to a crack shot.

Aeroplanes, although an incomparably larger target than a man, actually do not come within effective rifle range until they are 600 yards away. A good shot may hit a stationary man's head at 1000 yards, but he probably will waste his bullet if he fires at a plane at a range farther than 1000 yards. Even then the plane should not be more than 2000 feet from the ground.

The reason is not only the speed of the plane, but the fact that it is armoured. Few bullets will pierce a modern fighting plane if it is flying at above 2000 feet. The very fact that below this height can be fatal should a regiment of good shots be there, keeps a plane flying much higher thus decreasing the efficiency of its bombing, its machine gunning, and its terrorist tactics.

Aeroplanes which interest us most are those swooping low to bomb, or those flying low over the ground to spy out our position, or those that come screeching down in the dive. Providing you are not in ambush or helping hold a position in which it is not essential you should withhold your fire, here are the only guides known for aiming at aeroplanes: Firstly, remember the personal guide I've given you; it has never been in print. The idea of aiming ahead and counting the second or seconds before firing. With an aeroplane at close quarters, you have to be mighty quick. Otherwise, fix your sights at 500 yards if the plane is approaching. As a plane is very large and approaches so swiftly the sight fixing is practically for elevation alone. Now, planes come in two main ways. Flying towards or across your position or diving straight at you. If diving at you, aim straight at him immediately his wings tilt to come down at the dive. Continue rapid firing until he's lurched up and soared away. You can wheel around and keep blazing at his tail until he's out of range for if your aim is straight the bullet will catch him up.

Where a few hundred of you are waiting for him, the most effective fire would be a volley just when his nose was soaring up to turn away. Thus all his "belly" would be exposed to the closest range of your combined bullets. Have your sights aimed a couple of feet ahead of the tip of his nose. If he got away from such a volley he would be a lucky plane. Keep pumping shots into his tail, however, until he comes down or is out of range.

When a plane within effective range is flying towards or across your position within effective range (say 350 yards in height) aim a foot in front of its nose and keep the rifle muzzle travelling with it as you fire. Despite its speed the bullet must catch it somewhere for it is such a large target at that range. Remember, a bullet travels 600 yards in the first second.

If in the Regulars you should be the makings of an excellent shot by now. Otherwise you're all set for training into a pretty good guerrilla so far as rifle fire is concerned. Only practice shots, now, should be necessary for you to hit the head of a man at 1000 yards. You know all about direction, range finding, wind, distance, and aiming; from aiming at a crawling man through various speeds to aiming at an aeroplane.

Now we come to night shooting. It is different altogether to day-time work as you will easily realize. And is possible only at short ranges. In action, the targets would be the flashes of the enemy's rifles, or the ribbon of flame from a machine gun. You would pick out a flash opposite, wait for it, be all ready to locate it instantly it comes again, to mark it by some shadowy bush, or rock, or tree near it. Align your rifle, aim for it, and then when the next flash comes judge, without firing, whether your sights were directly set for it. Move your muzzle accordingly, be ready, then instantly the flash comes align your muzzle and fire.

The only other target, probably, would be "suspected" movement, or the problematical judgment that an enemy might be lying behind such or such an advantageous bush or log or other cover. Such shooting would really be "probing fire".

About the only visible target in night action under such circumstances would be "shadow men" advancing stealthily; advancing in short rushes, or coming at the charge, or the half guessed at, part shadow, figure of some badly placed outpost sentry. It may come in some unguarded sound made by a stealthy night sniper, or it may be the half guessed at, crawling shadows of a patrol. In any case you would aim exactly as you would if quite alone, and a single enemy or a number of them were stalking you, or stealthily walking along unsuspecting your ambush— as the case may be.

Unless, of course, your leader had given orders not to fire until his command, the shooting would be at short range and the ordinary 200 yard sight would be up. Aiming would depend upon light, upon time, and conditions at the moment. Such as whether you and the enemy were in timbered country and among shadows; whether he was coming towards you, and by waiting, you thought you could get a better shot, etc.

In any case, unless in bright moonlight with your enemy either silhouetted or out in the open, you would only have a momentarily appearing and reappearing shadow man to aim at. Your object of course would be, if possible, to wait until you had him in a "light" patch when his form would be more or less distinct. Then sight him not from low down as in daylight, but aim from the side as if to cut across him. Aim to the side of him, about the height of his belt. Soon as you've got the fore-sight within the U then slowly swing the rifle muzzle to "cut him". Immediately his shadow blackens out the sights—fire.

As you bring the rifle up beside him you get the elevation, then the sights in line and your eye sees open air away past the sights. As slowly you "cut him" with the muzzle the "open air" is of course blotted our and you "have him".

If you brought the rifle muzzle up from his feet, as you would in day, he and the sights and all would be shadow or blackness and you wouldn't know whether the sights were on him or a tree or rock or anywhere at all.

I'll have a little more to say on night fighting in *Sniping*, a booklet which will follow hard upon this one. Meanwhile, you've got the secret of aiming at night.

CHAPTER VIII
Hints from Experience:
Rapid Shooting

THINK over what has been written in the previous chapters. Read them again and again. There's a life-time's experience in them. There you will find the knowledge which, applied correctly by you, will quickly make you a crack rifle shot—granted actual practice. Only the authorities can give you the ammunition. They certainly should do so, for you are giving your services and possibly your life in return.

Now you may like to know a little about the simple mechanics, and various other points of a rifle. Nothing technical, for it is the use of the weapon you need urgently to know.

The rifle you will probably be issued with will be the S.M.L.E. (Short Magazine Lee-Enfield Rifle) Mark III. The magazine holds ten cartridges, in metal clips of five each. Another bullet can be carried in the breech or chamber as it is generally called. The weapon is simply operated by bolt action. There is a safety catch that locks the weapon against accidental firing should there be a cartridge in the chamber and the rifle set for firing. Use this safety catch if at any time your rifle is loaded and at full cock, otherwise you're liable to have an accident. But remember to release the safety catch when you wish to fire. I've vivid memories of an outpost attack. The Turks rushed us at dawn, it was a case of leaping up and firing at point blank range. One young trooper crouched frantically, snapping his trigger, but not firing a shot. When the hurly burly was over the shaking lad found he had not pulled back his safety catch. The miracle was that the oversight had not cost him his life. The same experience might easily befall you with a more unpleasant result should you forget that safety catch.

Get on the range as quickly as you can with your rifle. "Learn" the weapon; learn its peculiarities; make sure early that its mechanism, sights, and barrel are perfect. Keep it clean, with the mechanism just slightly oiled. The barrel should be new, but if it is an old one and becomes fouled you'll be advised to run the wire gauze through it. This gauze is supplied with the pull-through which, with an oil bottle is carried in a recess in the butt. Oil the gauze well before pulling it through otherwise it might scratch the rifling in the barrel. Before pulling a gauze through however, try pouring hot water down the barrel, emptying it down the breach. If it was impossible to get hot water then use cold, but dry the barrel thoroughly afterwards. The main cause of a rifle fouling is because the owner does not keep it clean. Hence, the chemicals in the explosive on combustion coat the barrel with film and grit. A speck or two of nickel casing may also be scratched off the bullet and adhere to the rifling as the bullet passes through. Boiling water will go a long way towards dissolving and loosening the refuse in a fouled barrel.

Clean your rifle after each shoot, for then any dirt in the barrel has not had time to become firmly set upon the rifling, and the pull-through will easily remove it. Put the pull-through in at the breach always. There is a golden rule to remember with a rifle barrel. If it shoots well, be satisfied; don't monkey about with it. Simply keep it clean and dry. When you use the pull-through be sure that the flannelette is dry. If you pull a moist rag through the barrel naturally it leaves a film of dampness inside which quickly turns to rust. When you have dried the barrel, run a slightly oiled rag through it. Be careful of your sights; although they are well protected, carelessness or rough handling might lead to them being knocked out of plumb.

Here are a few causes of bad shooting. Each is a fault which can be corrected. If you have mastered the aiming position already described, these faults should not trouble you:

(a)   A slight canting of the rifle. This of course puts the sights out of line.

(b)   Flinching at the moment of firing. With some men it also causes an upward movement of the muzzle with the result that the bullet flies high.

(c)   Not holding the elevation. This means that after the first few shots you are "dropping" the foresight. A common fault. Train yourself to remember that with every shot you take in all the full amount of foresight blade. Otherwise the bullet loses the correct elevation and falls low. It is better to have just a shade too much foresight than too little.

(d)   "Slanting sights." If the sights are not kept perfectly upright, if they incline the slightest degree to right or left, the bullet will fly right or left. Slanting sights mean that the marksman is not holding the rifle upright.

(e)   The trigger finger on the trigger when it should not be there. This is a serious fault and must not happen to you; if it does you may shoot your mate. Such an accident happens when a man touches the trigger of a loaded rifle before he is prepared to fire.

(f)   Flinching from "kick". The kick of a rifle is not much, and is no inconvenience if the weapon is correctly held. But if a man does not master the correct firing position then he cannot hold the rifle firmly enough, nor is the butt set firmly in the hollow of the shoulder. The rifle thus being loosely or uncomfortably held kicks and the firer, waiting for and expecting the kick next time, flinches and the bullet flies wide of the mark.

(g)   Bad and jerky trigger pressing. A common fault which has made many a man despair of ever shooting straight. The correct method has been explained already, so the fault should not trouble you. Never "flip at" or jerk the trigger, just pull it steadily when ready to fire. Practise trigger pressing for twenty minutes or so with an empty rifle at home. Spread yourself out comfortably in the firing position, then aim, and get your sights perfectly in line with correct elevation, just as if you were really aiming in earnest. Then press the trigger steadily and with perfect control. Such practice is a wonderful aid, as you will see in a rapidly increasing efficiency when you fire on the range. When you've got your grip and aimed, pause a moment and prove whether you have your trigger grip perfectly. Waggle your trigger finger. If you have to alter your hand or grip in the least, or if the rifle moves the faintest bit, the grip of your right hand is not correct. You should be able to move your trigger finger without affecting the remainder of your hand. That trigger finger has one especial job only and that is to fire the rifle correctly.

It should be able to do this job with perfect ease, quite independently of the rest of the hand.

You must know about this. It is used in beating off a charge, or quickly advancing troops, or in ambush upon a column of men. Rapid firing is the art of firing as rapidly and accurately as possible. Like ordinary or deliberate shooting there is a right way to go about it. An expert can fire up to thirty-five accurate shots a minute, but it takes doing. The number of rounds a man can accurately fire depends on his absolute mastery of the rifle and knowledge of this particular job.

In ordinary shooting you settle yourself comfortably; aim; fire. Then quietly pull back the bolt in the reloading, and steadily re-aim if necessary. But in rapid shooting your movements must be very quick and efficient, as nearly instantaneous as is humanly possible, while still with iron nerve aiming and shooting solid as a rock.

Your targets are running towards you, or you are firing at running men to your flank. If you fired, then jerked up your head, lowered your rifle, lifted right elbow and arm off the ground while reloading, then lifted the rifle again and aimed, the enemy would be within bayonet thrust of you before you had emptied your first clip of cartridges.

Hence, your object is to remain perfectly immovable with every part of your body that you can, while your eye and sights are fixed on the next oncoming target and you reload with what is practically only a determined flick of the right wrist.

We'll explain it this way. You are in the firing position; your eye is on the target; you fire, then eye and sights are instantly on the next oncoming target while no part of your body, except the right wrist, moves. This wrist instantly re-loads in the one swift movement while not disturbing rifle and right shoulder the slightest bit more than is necessary, the trigger finger immediately takes the first pull and you fire again.

That is the secret—the movement of the wrist, the one movement necessary.

Practice it at home. You will find it a bit difficult at first for your instinctive movements after firing will be: (1) to open your eyes, take deep breaths, raise your head with a satisfied feeling; (2) Lower the rifle to the floor thus taking the rifle not only from the shoulder and chin but moving both arms and probably elbows as well; (3) relax the whole body; (4) draw back the wrist, and all of the right arm in one wide, expansive movement of reloading; (5) go through a whole chapter of movements in taking aim again.

Just lie there a moment and imagine how much closer a berserk enemy would have got to you in that time. Imagine the cold glint of steel from his bayonet point. It's a nasty feeling when seen in earnest. I've seen it and, unless this war quickly goes a bit more our way, you'll see it too.

The knack of rapid firing then is to learn rapid reloading with one movement of the wrist; to switch back the knob of the bolt and as the empty shell flies out switch forward the bolt again.

Aim, fire, and try it, keeping eyes and entire body still in the firing position while you reload with fingers and wrist, making no movement of the body and as little movement of the right arm as possible.

You may need to lift your right elbow from the ground, and so lift up the rifle barrel as the right arm completely moves. If so, you must settle down for a new aim. Never mind. You will have learned a lot from that simple lesson; learned that you can reload without lowering the rifle, without moving the left arm, in fact without moving the body at all except the right arm. And all that time you have kept some sort of aim.

That one experiment is a great start. You only need to practise now and in an unbelievably short time you will be able to reload with one quick movement of the right wrist, possibly of the right elbow too, and your sighting will be but little disturbed.

Here are a few' points that will help you to reach perfection.

Your rifle bolt must be clean, and lightly oiled. Flick it back and forward with thumb and forefinger operating on the bolt knob. You'll quickly get the movement, and learn how much quicker and easier a clean, slightly oiled bolt will fly back, and return into place, than an unclean, stiff one. Hold your rifle in the firing position and work the bolt back and forward while aiming and keeping the rest of the body as immovable as possible. This will give you the "feel" of the movement.

Some excellent rapid shots do not even move the right elbow; others, equally as good, do. Practise until you have attained your own particular movement. You may find that your easiest and quickest movement is a slight one of the right elbow as the wrist flicks back the bolt, then the rifle barrel settles to the aim as the bolt shoots home and the elbow settles down again.

As the bolt snaps home the right hand automatically grips the small of the butt and the trigger finger coils around the trigger with the eye on the target and sights.

And now I'll suggest a slight alteration in the movement which, in my shooting was an improvement. It made the movement a shade faster and also did away with the energy, and slight movement necessary in the dropping of the bolt knob followed by the right hand dropping back to grip the Small of the butt and move the trigger finger around the trigger. Instead of gripping the small of the butt with the right hand I'd grip the bolt knob between thumb and forefinger (trigger finger) then with one up and back, forward and down movement eject the empty cartridge and reload and instantly my middle finger was around the trigger with thumb still pressed down on the bolt knob. I fired like that; there was no shifting of the hand back around the small of the butt. At the same time it seemed easier to keep the rifle barrel aligned or automatically pick up the next target. Try this method; it may suit you too.

In every phase of rifle fire, if you can pick up some little trick that suits you individually and improves your shooting, then do so by all means. The one urgent object is to learn to shoot straight-as straight as it is humanly possible for you to shoot.

CHAPTER IX
Snap Shooting

REMEMBER that though rapid fire is more difficult to learn than deliberate shooting still it is a lot your way. It is used at "full time" targets, such as men or bodies of men running towards you, or at a body of massed men who may be marching, or stationary, or momentarily clumped together. Your target will be a full-grown man, probably in the open, and very probably at close range. Hence you have lots to "come and go on"; there is plenty of him to hit. If you and your comrades have trained yourselves to rapid shooting and mentally remain cool you will hit many of those targets before they get within bomb and bayonet reach. If you are a band of good, cool shots they will never get to close quarters, not unless they are in absolutely overwhelming numbers. But you must be good shots.

In rapid shooting the body and left arm although stationary still help to hold the rifle in position. We will consider that you have mastered the bolt action; that, as the bolt clicks home, you are aiming and could fire one second later.

It is practice that does this, practice in aiming during deliberate shooting. You have learned when the target is correctly balanced and exactly at that moment you press the trigger.

This practice is what counts in rapid shooting, for the rifle is at the aim all the time and your practised eye has never left the target, or has picked up another one and automatically focuses foresight on to target and then rearsight even while you begin to press the trigger. Fire immediately, don't wait or you'll go off the target.

There is yet another form of shooting—snap shooting. This is when you see, or expect an enemy to appear at any moment. Then he pops back. Or he appears running to cover but is only visible for a few moments. You can expect to get two shots at him, possibly three. After which you can rest your rifle and be on the alert again.

This shooting is a mixture of deliberate, and rapid. You may have drawn a "bead" on the spot where you expect him to appear, hence your first shot is more or less deliberate. You miss, and he dashes on to further cover so that your next shot is a snap shot. If you are used to rapid shooting it is easy. You have reloaded, aimed and fired again within a couple of seconds. If you have not practised rapid shooting your target disappears before you can get the next shot in.

Snap shooting may be necessary in this way. Say you are alone, or in line with a number of others. Facing you 1000 or more or less yards away is a line of the enemy, very cautiously advancing. You can see nothing but previously have noted a spot where a man has taken cover. You draw a bead on that spot—ready. He appears and dashes forward to flop down again under cover. If you've been quick and accurate you may have got him. Anyway, you're still in the firing position with your eye to the sights and line of target while the wrist flicks a new bullet into the chamber. Another figure suddenly appears, bounding forward. Your sights swing to him, you aim and fire just as he is in the act of flopping down. That is snap shooting.

Here's a point or two in snap shooting. Keep on the job, but above all, keep calm, be confident. If you let yourself get flurried, or the least bit excited, then you must miss. Because you only have two or three seconds to aim and fire. Your target will be doing the moving, if you allow a mental nervousness or excitement to move you in the least.

Remember your elevation. In this "cat watching- for- a-mouse" type of shooting you are very liable to forget elevation, and thus shoot low. Always automatically remember to take a full foresight. As to range you should have that accurately if you've fired before, for you see the dust from previous shots. If it happens to be a windy day, make due allowance for wind, exactly as explained in chapter six.

At every chance, rest your arms. Remember that it means an increasing strain on the arms to hold the rifle unnecessarily.

The golden rule under all circumstances to remember is: Act quickly when necessary and on all occasions keep cool. Then nothing can prevent you from becoming a deadly shot.

THE DESERT COLUMN
An Australian Trooper in Gallipoli and Palestine

ION IDRIESS

With a Foreword by General Sir Harry Chauvel, G.C.M.G., K.C.B., late Commanding the Desert Mounted Corps.

Scotsman (Edinburgh) :-"His book, valuable as a document of war, is an absorbing example of descriptive reporting .... Difficulties and dangers, escapades and escapes, fill the pages of the book with excitement."

W. Farmer Whyte in the *Daily Mail* (Brisbane) :-"In *The Desert Column*, which has brought the author letters from over half the globe, we have a War Diary which, for its stark realism and colourful descriptions, has certainly not been surpassed."

Natal Mercury (South Africa) :-"One of the most vivid pieces of war narrative that has ever been written .... "

Cavalry Journal (London) :-"Personality, accuracy, and a fine spirit breathe through its pages. It can be heartily recommended to all cavalry readers."

Montreal Daily Star (Canada) :-"The author is a born writer, and he has missed nothing of the drama, the comedy, the tragedy, and the intense humanity of the scene."

New Zealand Magazine:-"His book is a perfect thing in its way .... It is as animated and realistic as a cinematograph film. *The Desert Column* deserves shelf room in every New Zealand home."

Now in its 26th edition, 330 pages, available from ETT Imprint.

DRUMS OF MER

ION IDRIESS

With Foreword by Wm H. MacFarlane, Mission Priest, Torres Strait Administrator of the Diocese of Carpentaria.

Professor T. G. Tucker, Litt.D. (Camb.), Hon. Litt.D. (Dublin), writes :-"Apart from his evident knowledge of the natives and their customs, Idriess has a graphic power greater than that of any writer whom I have read for years. His accounts of a battle of canoes, the wreck of a flotilla, and other events, are the finest things of the kind that anyone out here has produced."

Christchurch Times (N.Z.) :-"Idriess's Masterpiece. To enter into the life of a savage race of a bygone age, and to make that life spring into renewed reality, so that the blood runs hot and cold in response to its splendour and its degrada¬tion-this is" the feat, almost an unparalleled feat, that has been achieved by Ion Idriess in *Drums of Mer* .... Idriess must now rank as the most brilliant star in the literary galaxy of Australia, and world fame for him can only be a question of time."

Sydney Mail :-"In dramatic appeal it is superior to *Gold-Dust and Ashes* and *The Desert Column* ... that should be sufficient."

Pacific Islands Monthly:-"Mr Idriess, in the telling of his story, displays sheer genius. There is something here for the scientist, the historian, the geographer, the beauty lover, and the student of the occult. *Drums of Mer* is not only a story, it is an invaluable addition to the historical records of the Pacific Islands."

The Argus (Melbourne) :-"He has seized upon the most colourful aspects of this decayed civilization before it has been completely lost to living memory, and has dramatized them with his uncanny gift for realistic narrative writing."

Now in its 23th edition, 284 pages, available from ETT Imprint.

THE YELLOW JOSS

ION IDRIESS

With Foreword by Tony Grey. Illustrated.

Sydney Morning Herald :-"The Booya is a masterpiece of the weird and terrible. But of all the tales "The Castaway" has most power and surely merits a place with similar episodes in Conrad. Mr Idriess is adept in working up the feelings of his readers to a pitch of expectancy ... Here the excitement is terrific."

The Herald (Melbourne) :-"Every one of these tales bears the impress of truth. Anybody who lets unreasoned prejudice against short stories deter them from reading this book is missing a treat."

The Sun (Sydney) :-"Idriess tells a good story. These come from another world, a primitive and violent world, where things that seem fantastic and incredible to dwellers in the Australian cities are commonplaces of life."

Queensland Times :-"He has the happy knack of being able to blend truth and fiction in such a way that even commonplace things assume an important role and have definite and impelling force."

Woman's Budget (Sydney) :-"They give a clearer insight into his varied and adventurous life than anything he has previously written."

Honi Soit (University of Sydney) :-"Rich humour enlivens the book, particularly where the exploits of one 'Scandalous' Graham are concerned."

Producers' Review (Brisbane) :-"The name of Ion Idriess has become a household word ... as a maker of short stories he has lost none of his flair for tale-telling. Indeed we prefer this style."

Now in its 10th edition, 210 pages, available from ETT Imprint.

PROSPECTING FOR GOLD

ION IDRIESS

From the Dish to the Hydraulic Plant, and from the Dolly to the Stamper Battery. With chapters on Prospecting for Opal, Tin, and other Minerals; and a chapter on Prospecting for Oil, by Dr W. G. Woolnough, F.G.S., Geologist to the Commonwealth of Australia. Illustrated.

This book, written by a prospector with a lifetime's experience, will save the new chum gold-seeker much labour and time and disappointment, and will teach the old hand many a payable wrinkle.

Dr W. G. Woolnough (Geologist to the Commonwealth of Australia) :-"Your hints should be invaluable to all, beginners and experienced men alike."

Canadian Mining and Metallurgical Bulletin:-"The volume will arouse the reader's interest at the outset and hold it to the end."

Queensland Government Mining Journal :-"It tersely sums up a lifetime's knowledge gained at first hand acquired by a man well equipped to pass his experience on to others."

Engineering and Mining Journal (New York) :-"This book is replete with good methods, described simply. Lack of space forbids quoting the terse directions."

Rabaul Times (New Guinea) :-"Invaluable. Each bit of advice and information is practical, as it comes from an old-time miner himself."

Now in its 20th edition, 190 pages, available from ETT Imprint.

LASSETER'S DIARY

Transcribed with Mud-Maps

Harold Bell Lasseter had always claimed he had found an immense reef of gold hundreds of miles west of Alice Springs. In 1930, with Australia in the grip of Depression, a privately funded expedition led by Fred Blakeley, accompanied Lasseter in an attempt to relocate the reef. Blakeley left Lasseter at Ililba, and Lasseter continued his trek towards the Olgas with a dingo shooter and their camels. Lasseter continued to be introspective and brood, prompting Lasseter to go off alone with two camels.

In March 1931 an expedition led by bushman Bob Buck found Lasseter's body at Winter's Glen, and his diary at Hull's Creek, wherein it describes how after his camels bolted, he was alone in the desert, encountering a group of nomadic Aboriginals who offered offer him food and shelter. Blind, exhausted and dying, Lasseter made one last attempt to walk from Hull's Creek to Uluru.

The diary was purchased by Ion Idriess from Lasseter's widow in 1931, and from it he wrote the best-seller Lasseter's Last Ride. Tom Thompson has transcribed the diary with its original mud-maps, including those not in the diary itself and Lasseter's drawings.

First edition, 90 pages, available from ETT Imprint.